First printing: April 2017
Second printing: November 2017

Copyright © 2017 by Answers in Genesis–USA. All rights reserved. No part of this book may be used or reproduced in any manner whatsoever without written permission of the publisher, except in the case of brief quotations in articles and reviews. For information write:
Master Books®, P.O. Box 726,
Green Forest, AR 72638
Master Books® is a division of the New Leaf Publishing Group, Inc.

ISBN: 978-1-68344-033-8
ISBN: 978-1-61458-293-9 (digital)
Library of Congress Number: 2017902899

Written by Tim Chaffey
Illustrated by Colin Dyer

Scripture referenced in this book is based on the New King James Version, New International Version, English Standard Version, New American Standard Bible, and the New English Translation.

Please consider requesting that a copy of this volume be purchased by your local library system.

Printed in China

Please visit our website for other great titles:
www.masterbooks.com

For information regarding author interviews, please contact the publicity department at (870) 438-5288.

MB
Master Books®
A Division of New Leaf Publishing Group
www.masterbooks.com

THE ILLUSTRATED GOSPEL

searching for Truth

CAMPUS LIFE

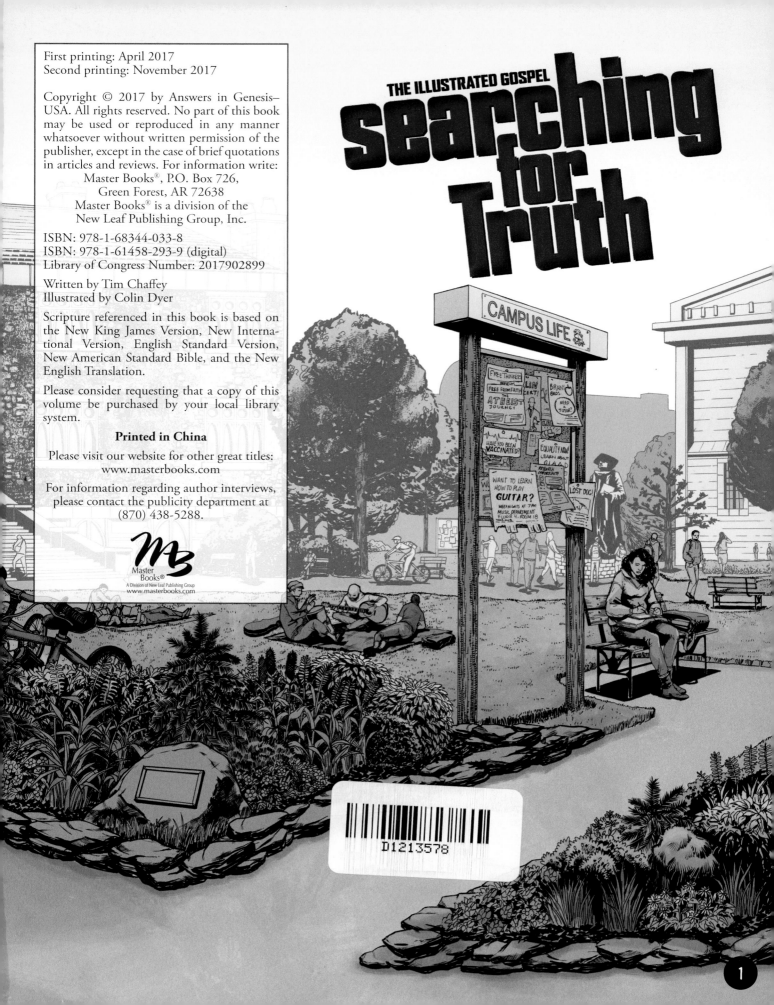

D1213578

1

3

ALL 02
I BELIEVE THE BIBLE IS TRUE AND THAT JESUS IS THE ONLY WAY TO HEAVEN.
NOTICE:
NEXT WEEK'S LECTURE HAS BEEN RE-SCHEDULED.
DATE WILL BE TBD
—CHEERS

ALL SCRIPTURE IS GIVEN BY INSPIRATION OF GOD, AND IS PROFITABLE FOR DOCTRINE, FOR REPROOF, FOR CORRECTION, FOR INSTRUCTION IN RIGHTEOUSNESS, THAT THE MAN OF GOD MAY BE COMPLETE, THOROUGHLY EQUIPPED FOR EVERY GOOD WORK.

2 TIMOTHY 3:16-17

HMM. NO ERRORS? A CONSISTENT MESSAGE?

THE DOCTRINE OF INERRANCY

ANDRE EXPRESSED AN IDEA KNOWN AS THE DOCTRINE OF INERRANCY. IN ITS MOST BASIC FORMULATION, THIS TEACHING STATES THAT THE BIBLE, BOTH OLD AND NEW TESTAMENTS, WERE WRITTEN WITHOUT ERROR IN THE ORIGINAL MANUSCRIPTS. THIS IDEA ONLY APPLIES TO THE COPIES INSOFAR AS THEY ARE FAITHFUL TO THE ORIGINAL WRITINGS.

UNIQUE CHARACTERISTICS OF THE BIBLE:

~ THE BIBLE IS A COLLECTION OF 66 BOOKS.

~ THE 39 BOOKS OF THE OLD TESTAMENT WERE ORIGINALLY WRITTEN IN HEBREW, WITH THE EXCEPTION OF SOME SMALL SECTIONS OF ARAMAIC, MOST NOTABLY IN EZRA AND DANIEL.

~ THE 27 BOOKS OF THE NEW TESTAMENT WERE ORIGINALLY WRITTEN IN GREEK.

~ THE BIBLE WAS WRITTEN BY AT LEAST 40 DIFFERENT AUTHORS, MANY OF WHOM WERE EYEWITNESSES, OVER A SPAN OF AT LEAST 1500 YEARS FROM THREE CONTINENTS (ASIA, AFRICA, AND EUROPE).

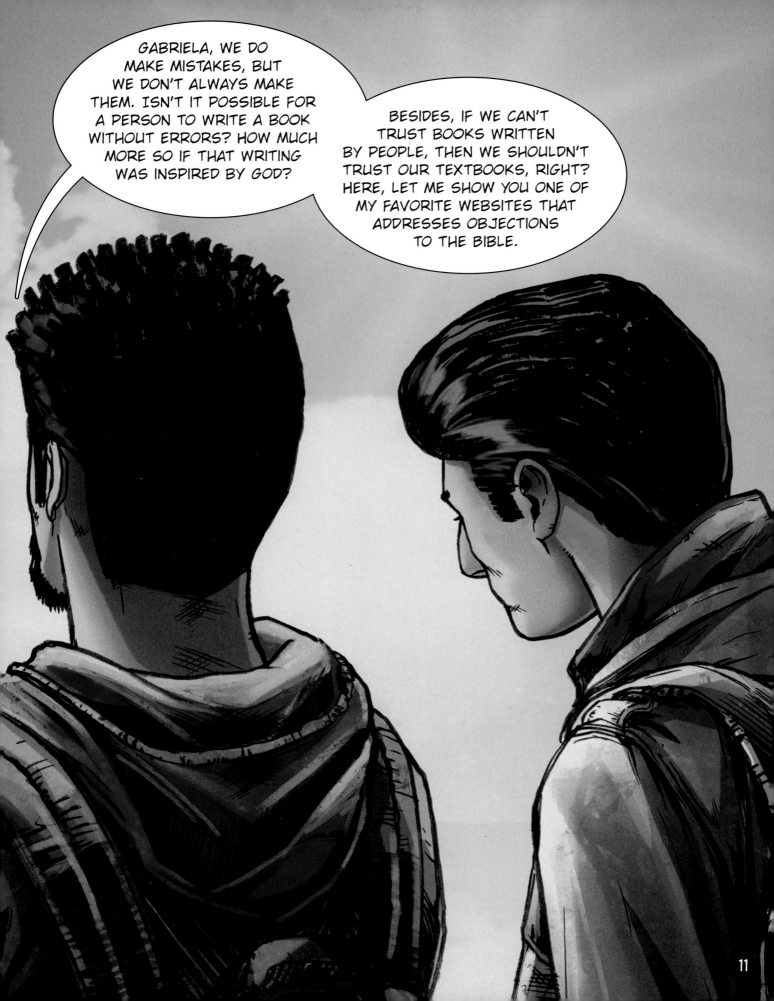

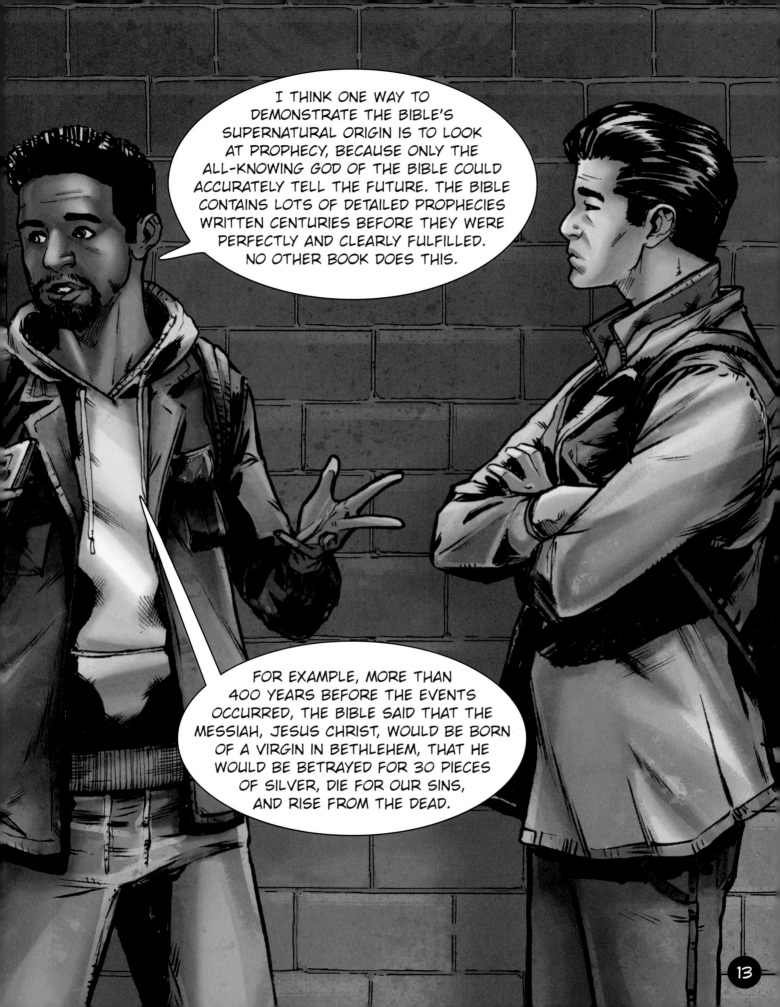

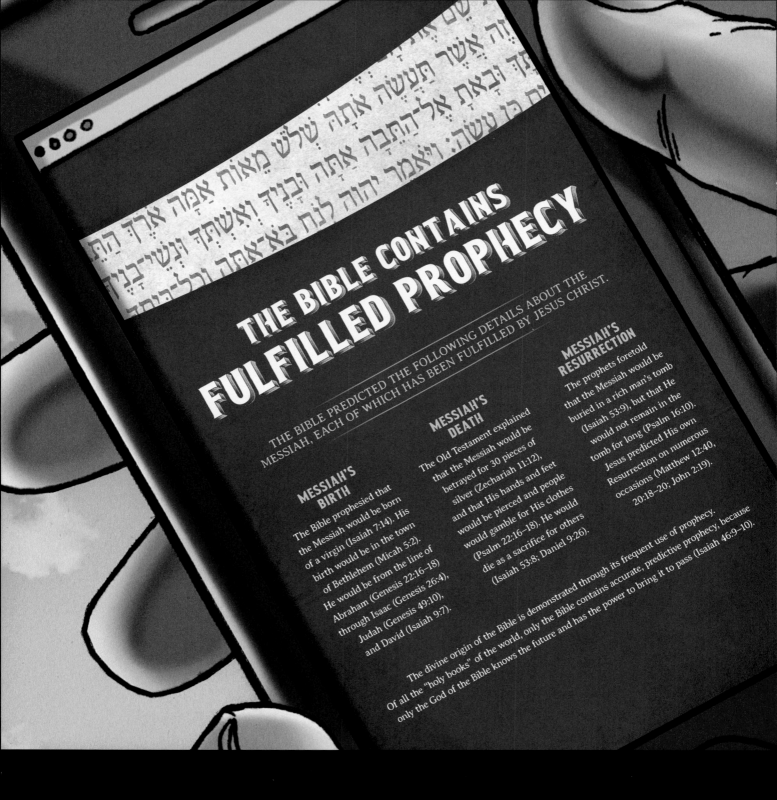

THE BIBLE CONTAINS FULFILLED PROPHECY

THE BIBLE PREDICTED THE FOLLOWING DETAILS ABOUT THE MESSIAH, EACH OF WHICH HAS BEEN FULFILLED BY JESUS CHRIST.

MESSIAH'S BIRTH

The Bible prophesied that the Messiah would be born of a virgin (Isaiah 7:14). His birth would be in the town of Bethlehem (Micah 5:2). He would be from the line of Abraham (Genesis 22:16–18) through Isaac (Genesis 26:4), Judah (Genesis 49:10), and David (Isaiah 9:7).

MESSIAH'S DEATH

The Old Testament explained that the Messiah would be betrayed for 30 pieces of silver (Zechariah 11:12), and that His hands and feet would be pierced and people would gamble for His clothes (Psalm 22:16–18). He would die as a sacrifice for others (Isaiah 53:8; Daniel 9:26).

MESSIAH'S RESURRECTION

The prophets foretold that the Messiah would be buried in a rich man's tomb (Isaiah 53:9), but that He would not remain in the tomb for long (Psalm 16:10). Jesus predicted His own Resurrection on numerous occasions (Matthew 12:40, 20:18–20; John 2:19).

The divine origin of the Bible is demonstrated through its frequent use of prophecy. Of all the "holy books" of the world, only the Bible contains accurate, predictive prophecy, because only the God of the Bible knows the future and has the power to bring it to pass (Isaiah 46:9–10).

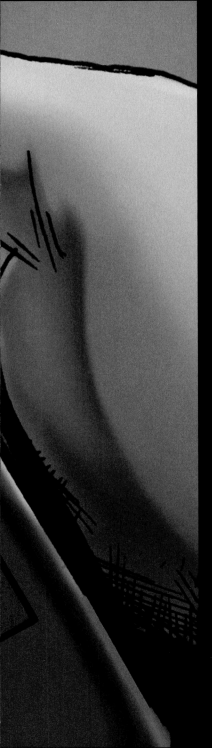

MESSIAH'S BIRTH

THEREFORE THE LORD HIMSELF WILL GIVE YOU A SIGN:
BEHOLD, THE VIRGIN SHALL CONCEIVE AND BEAR A SON,
AND SHALL CALL HIS NAME IMMANUEL.

ISAIAH 7:14

BUT YOU, BETHLEHEM EPHRATHAH,
THOUGH YOU ARE LITTLE AMONG THE THOUSANDS OF JUDAH,
YET OUT OF YOU SHALL COME FORTH TO ME
THE ONE TO BE RULER IN ISRAEL,
WHOSE GOINGS FORTH ARE FROM OF OLD,
FROM EVERLASTING.

MICAH 5:2

MESSIAH'S DEATH

THEN I SAID TO THEM, "IF IT IS AGREEABLE TO YOU, GIVE ME
MY WAGES; AND IF NOT, REFRAIN." SO THEY WEIGHED OUT
FOR MY WAGES THIRTY PIECES OF SILVER.

ZECHARIAH 11:12

FOR DOGS HAVE SURROUNDED ME;
THE CONGREGATION OF THE WICKED HAS ENCLOSED ME.
THEY PIERCED MY HANDS AND MY FEET.

PSALM 22:16

MESSIAH'S RESURRECTION

AND THEY MADE HIS GRAVE WITH THE WICKED—
BUT WITH THE RICH AT HIS DEATH,
BECAUSE HE HAD DONE NO VIOLENCE,
NOR WAS ANY DECEIT IN HIS MOUTH.

ISAIAH 53:9

FOR YOU WILL NOT LEAVE MY SOUL IN SHEOL,
NOR WILL YOU ALLOW YOUR HOLY ONE TO SEE CORRUPTION.

PSALM 16:10

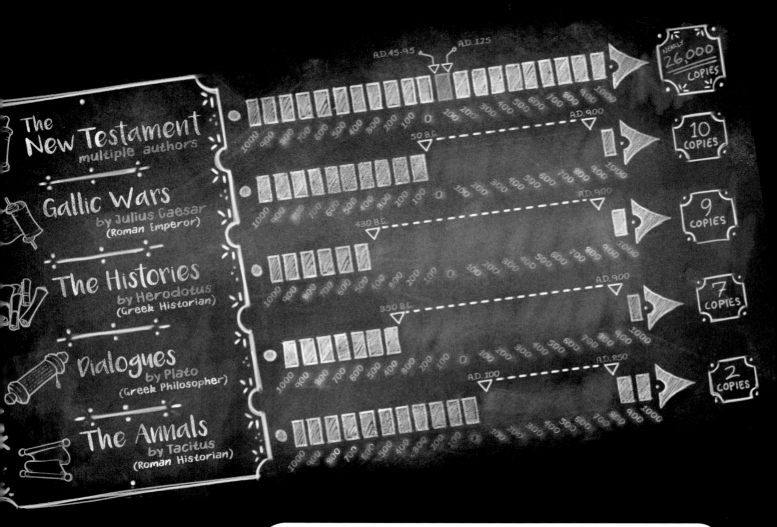

THE "HILL OF BEANS" VIDEO CONTRASTS THE MANUSCRIPT EVIDENCE FOR THE NEW TESTAMENT WITH THE MANUSCRIPT EVIDENCE FOR OTHER ANCIENT WRITINGS. EACH ROW INCLUDES THE DATE OF AUTHORSHIP FOLLOWED BY THE DATE OF THE EARLIEST COPY.

TO WATCH THE VIDEO, AND TO LEARN MORE ABOUT THIS TOPIC, PLEASE VISIT WWW.ARKENCOUNTER.COM/BEANS.

THE IMAGES BELOW AND ON THE NEXT TWO PAGES ARE FROM A SLIDESHOW THAT GABRIELA VIEWS WHILE STUDYING IN THE LIBRARY. THEY REPRESENT A SMALL FRACTION OF SCIENTIFIC AND HISTORICAL EVIDENCES CONSISTENT WITH THE BIBLE.

SCIENTIFIC | **ACCURACY**

RADIOCARBON DATING

Radiocarbon in fossil wood, shells, bones, coal, and diamonds said to be millions of years old reveals that these items are less than 100,000 years old.

HISTORICAL | **ACCURACY**

TEL DAN STELE

This ninth century BC inscription refers to the dynasty of King David, refuting the common claim of critics that David was a legend invented by Israelites centuries later.

DINOSAUR SOFT TISSUE

Several dinosaur fossils, alleged to be over 65 million years old, contain soft tissue, DNA, and red blood cells, but these biological materials are known to decay rapidly.

SHORT-TERM COMETS

Thought to last for fewer than 10,000 years, the existence of short-term comets is consistent with the biblical age of the earth.

EARTH'S MAGNETIC FIELD

Based on its current decay rate, earth's magnetic field can be no older than 20,000 years old.

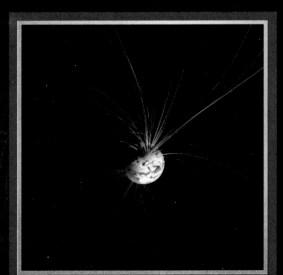

SENNACHERIB'S PRISM

Written around 691 BC, this clay prism confirms Sennacherib's failed siege of Jerusalem as described in 2 Kings, 2 Chronicles, and Isaiah.

PILATE STONE

Carved limestone found in Caesarea in 1961 that confirms the governorship of Pilate over Judea during the time of Christ.

NAZARETH INSCRIPTION

Edict of Emperor Claudius from AD 40s demonstrating the Christian belief in Christ's Resurrection had rapidly spread throughout the Roman Empire.

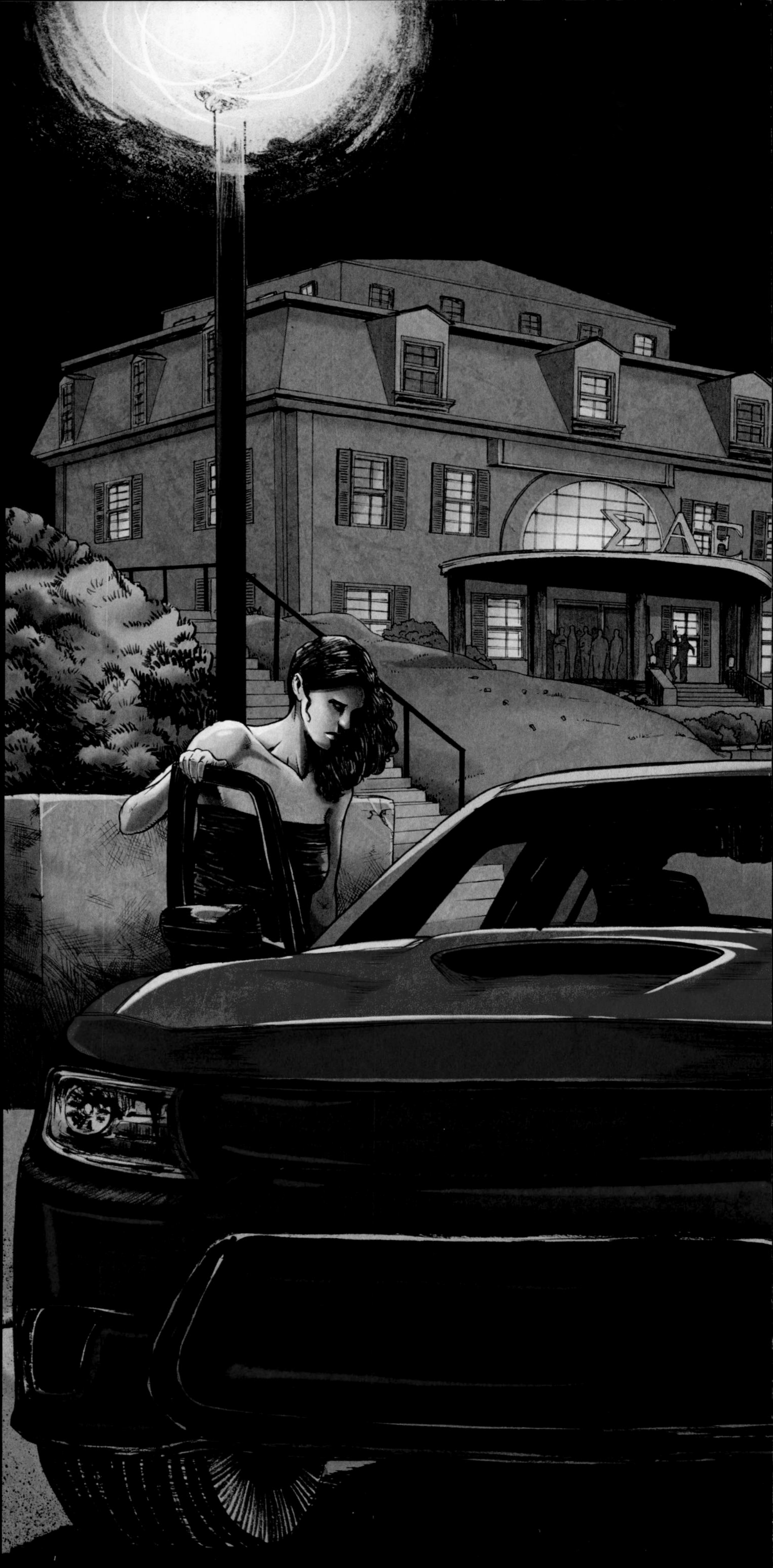
A FEW HOURS LATER...

BANG!

THE BIBLE TELLS US
THAT MEN HAD BECOME
EXCEEDINGLY WICKED—
THEY THOUGHT OF EVIL
CONTINUALLY—SO GOD
PLANNED TO FLOOD THE
EARTH AND WIPE THEM OUT.
HE TOLD NOAH TO BUILD AN
ARK AND TO PUT A DOOR
IN ITS SIDE. WHEN GOD
SHUT THE ARK'S DOOR IT
ILLUSTRATED HIS JUSTICE
AND HIS MERCY.

YOU SEE, THE WICKED WORLD OUTSIDE OF THE ARK WOULD PERISH. THOSE IN THE ARK, NOAH'S FAMILY, WERE SPARED. THAT ARK DOOR SERVES AS A PICTURE OF SOMETHING FAR GREATER, AS DO OTHER DOORS MENTIONED IN THE BIBLE.

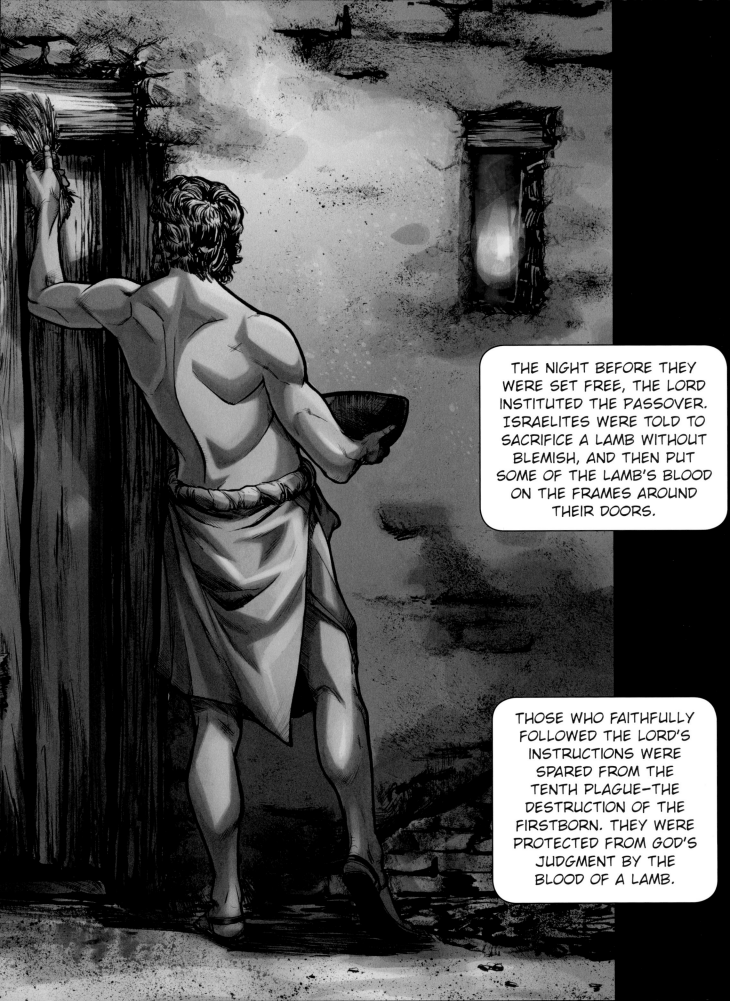

THE NIGHT BEFORE THEY WERE SET FREE, THE LORD INSTITUTED THE PASSOVER. ISRAELITES WERE TOLD TO SACRIFICE A LAMB WITHOUT BLEMISH, AND THEN PUT SOME OF THE LAMB'S BLOOD ON THE FRAMES AROUND THEIR DOORS.

THOSE WHO FAITHFULLY FOLLOWED THE LORD'S INSTRUCTIONS WERE SPARED FROM THE TENTH PLAGUE—THE DESTRUCTION OF THE FIRSTBORN. THEY WERE PROTECTED FROM GOD'S JUDGMENT BY THE BLOOD OF A LAMB.

NEARLY 500 YEARS AFTER MOSES, KING SOLOMON BUILT THE FIRST TEMPLE IN JERUSALEM. TWO DOORS WERE PLACED AT THE ENTRANCE TO THE INNER SANCTUARY WHERE GOD'S PRESENCE WAS.

THE ISRAELITES WERE ABLE TO TEMPORARILY HAVE THEIR SINS COVERED THROUGH THE SACRIFICE OF A GOAT, AND THUS RECEIVE GOD'S MERCY. THOUGH THE BLOOD OF THESE ANIMALS COULD NEVER TAKE AWAY MAN'S SIN, THEY POINTED FORWARD TO THE MOST IMPORTANT SACRIFICE OF ALL. JESUS OBTAINED ETERNAL REDEMPTION FOR US THROUGH HIS ONCE FOR ALL SINLESS OFFERING OF HIMSELF TO GOD.

BECAUSE
US FRO
THE CERE
HIGH P
ENTER
ONCE A Y
SACRIFICE
OF TH

BECAUSE EACH OF US HAS SINNED AGAINST GOD, WE NEED HIS FORGIVENESS, BUT THE BLOOD OF ANIMALS COULD NEVER TAKE AWAY OUR SINS. WE NEEDED A PERFECT SUBSTITUTE TO DIE IN OUR PLACE. FOR GOD SO LOVED THE WORLD, THAT HE SENT HIS SON, JESUS CHRIST, TO BECOME A MAN TO PAY FOR OUR SINS THROUGH HIS SACRIFICIAL DEATH ON THE CROSS. JESUS CHRIST, THE LAMB OF GOD, IS OUR PASSOVER WHOSE BLOOD CAN TAKE AWAY ALL OF OUR SINS.

THREE DAYS AFTER BEING CRUCIFIED, JESUS CHRIST ROSE FROM THE DEAD JUST AS HE PROMISED. ON THAT MORNING, AN ANGEL DESCENDED FROM HEAVEN AND ROLLED BACK THE STONE FROM THE DOOR OF THE TOMB... "DO NOT BE AFRAID, FOR I KNOW THAT YOU SEEK JESUS WHO WAS CRUCIFIED. HE IS NOT HERE; FOR HE IS RISEN, AS HE SAID" (MATTHEW 28:2-6).

THIS SPECTACULAR MIRACLE CONFIRMED THAT JE
CHRIST WAS EXACTLY WHO HE CLAIMED TO BE
THE SON OF GOD. THE RESURRECTION ALSO
DEMONSTRATED HIS POWER OVER DEATH,
GUARANTEEING THE HOPE OF ETERNAL LIFE TO
WHO REPENT OF THEIR SINS AND BELIEVE IN H

THE LAST TWO DOORS ARE MENTIONED IN THE FAMOUS SERMON ON THE MOUNT. JESUS SAID, "ENTER BY THE NARROW GATE; FOR WIDE THE GATE AND BROAD IS THE WAY THAT LEADS TO DESTRUCTION, AND THERE ARE MANY WHO GO IN BY IT. BECAUSE NARROW IS THE GATE AND DIFFICULT IS THE WAY WHICH LEADS TO LIFE, AND THERE ARE FEW WHO FIND IT" (MATTHEW 7:13-14).

SEVERAL DAYS LATER...

DING!

DING!

DING!

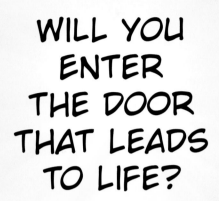

WILL YOU ENTER THE DOOR THAT LEADS TO LIFE?

WHAT WILL YOU DO WITH JESUS CHRIST?
YOUR ANSWER TO THAT QUESTION HAS
ETERNAL CONSEQUENCES.

EACH OF US IS GUILTY OF SINNING AGAINST
OUR HOLY CREATOR.
BECAUSE HE IS HOLY, GOD MUST JUDGE SIN.
TAKE AN HONEST LOOK AT YOUR LIFE.
HAVE YOU EVER LIED,
STOLEN ANYTHING,
DISRESPECTED YOUR PARENTS,
OR FAILED TO HONOR GOD?
IF SO, THEN YOU ARE A SINNER IN NEED OF A SAVIOR.

THERE WAS ONE DOOR INTO THE ARK
THAT SAVED NOAH AND HIS FAMILY FROM THE FLOOD.
SIMILARLY, THERE IS ONLY ONE "DOOR" THAT CAN SAVE US
FROM ETERNAL JUDGMENT. JESUS CHRIST IS THAT DOOR.
HE IS THE ONLY WAY TO BE SAVED FROM SIN.

THE BIBLE STATES THAT
NOW IS THE DAY OF SALVATION
(2 CORINTHIANS 6:2). IF YOU HAVE NOT ALREADY
DONE SO, WILL YOU TURN FROM YOUR SINS AND
CALL ON THE RISEN LORD TO SAVE YOU?

ENTER THE ONLY DOOR THAT LEADS TO ETERNAL LIFE TODAY.

FOR THE WAGES OF SIN IS DEATH, BUT THE GIFT OF GOD IS ETERNAL LIFE
IN CHRIST JESUS OUR LORD (ROMANS 6:23).

רֶם וְגַם אֶת־...
גוּף הַשָּׁמַיִם כִּי נִחַמְתִּי כִּי עֲשִׂיתִם: וְנֹחַ מָצָא חֵן...
כָּל־בָּשָׂר בָּא לְפָנַי כִּי־מָלְאָה הָאָרֶץ חָמָס מִפְּנֵיהֶם...
הַיּוֹם וּשְׁלֹשִׁים תַּעֲשֶׂהָ: וַאֲנִי הִנְנִי מֵבִיא אֶת־הַמַּבּ...
אֵלֶיךָ לְהַחֲיוֹת ... מִכֹּל יָבֹאוּ
מֵעוֹף הַשָּׁמַיִם

THE BIBLE IS GOD'S WORD

WHAT DOES IT MEAN THAT THE BIBLE'S WORDS ARE FROM GOD?

FULLY INSPIRED

"God-breathed." This term is used in 2 Timothy 3:16 to describe Scripture. This means that God moved and guided the authors of the Bible as they wrote. At the same time, this process allowed the writers to utilize their own styles and personalities.

AUTHORITATIVE

The words of the Bible ultimately come from the God who knows everything and who cannot lie. Therefore, it is authoritative in every subject it addresses, whether it is discussing scientific issues, history, geography, or any matter of faith and practice.

WITHOUT ERROR

Since the Bible is the Word of God, and since God cannot make mistakes, then it follows that the Bible does not contain errors. This teaching, known as the doctrine of inerrancy, applies to the original manuscripts

בְּרָאתִי מֵעַל פְּנֵי הָאֲדָמָה ... הַנְּפִלִים הָיוּ בָאָ...

...שְׁחִית כָּל־בָּשָׂר אָדָם עַד־בְּהֵמָה עַד־רֶ...

...פְּנֵי הָאֲדָמָה מֵאָדָם עַד־בְּהֵמָה עַד־דֶ...

...דַּרְכּוֹ עַל־הָאָרֶץ: וַיֹּאמֶר אֱלֹהִים...

THE BIBLE IS
UNIQUE & UNIFIED

THE BIBLE IS UNIQUE AMONG ALL THE BOOKS IN THE WORLD.

WRITTEN BY OVER
40
DIFFERENT WRITERS
including shepherds, kings, priests, scholars, fishermen, and prophets.

FLAWED HEROES
Most sacred writings hide the faults of their heroes, but the Bible does not do this. For example, King David committed adultery and tried to cover it up by having the woman's husband killed.

WRITTEN OVER A SPAN OF
1500
YEARS
from three different continents and in three different languages.

THE BIBLE'S MESSAGE IS UNIFIED THROUGHOUT ITS 66 BOOKS.

GENRES
The Bible remains unified in its message even though it displays a wide variety of literary styles: Genesis is primarily historical narrative, the Psalms are poetry, and the New Testament contains personal letters and predictive prophecy.

PURPOSES
The Bible maintains perfect unity despite the fact that its authors had different purposes in writing: Moses traced his people's history, David composed songs for worship, and Paul instructed churches to hold on to sound doctrine.

EMOTIONS
The Bible exhibits amazing consistency; still its writers express a broad range of powerful emotions: some Psalms vent intense anger, Lamentations conveys great sorrow, and Romans displays exhilarating joy in God's salvation.

אֵמָּה רַחְבָּהּ וּשְׁלֹשִׁים אֵלֹהִים אֶת־הָ...
...ל־הַחַי מִכָּל־בָּשָׂר...אֵמָּה קוֹמָתָהּ וְהִנֵּה נַשְׁחָ...

THE BIBLE HAS BEEN FAITHFULLY PASSED DOWN

IS THE BIBLE JUST A COPY OF A COPY?

This common objection to the accuracy of the Bible is based on a misunderstanding of how the Bible has been handed down to us.

The scribes who copied Scripture took great care in their work. Accuracy was ensured by a number of safeguards, including the counting of the number of letters in a line and on a page. Minor variations exist between certain manuscripts, but thanks to the abundance of early texts and fragments, we can ascertain the original wording in nearly every case.

AMAZING CONSISTENCY ACROSS CENTURIES

The discovery of the Dead Sea Scrolls in 1947 provides one remarkable example of how faithfully God's Word has been preserved.

The earliest complete Hebrew manuscript of the Old Testament, the Leningrad Codex, dates to the early eleventh century AD. The Dead Sea Scrolls were written more than 1000 years earlier, before the time of Christ. Other than variations in spelling and style, there is extraordinary consistency between these two sources, a fact that contradicts the critics' claims that the Bible has repeatedly been altered.

THE BIBLE CONTAINS FULFILLED PROPHECY

THE BIBLE PREDICTED THE FOLLOWING DETAILS ABOUT THE MESSIAH, EACH OF WHICH HAS BEEN FULFILLED BY JESUS CHRIST.

MESSIAH'S BIRTH

The Bible prophesied that the Messiah would be born of a virgin (Isaiah 7:14). His birth would be in the town of Bethlehem (Micah 5:2). He would be from the line of Abraham (Genesis 22:16–18) through Isaac (Genesis 26:4), Judah (Genesis 49:10), and David (Isaiah 9:7).

MESSIAH'S DEATH

The Old Testament explained that the Messiah would be betrayed for 30 pieces of silver (Zechariah 11:12), and that His hands and feet would be pierced and people would gamble for His clothes (Psalm 22:16–18). He would die as a sacrifice for others (Isaiah 53:8; Daniel 9:26).

MESSIAH'S RESURRECTION

The prophets foretold that the Messiah would be buried in a rich man's tomb (Isaiah 53:9), but that He would not remain in the tomb for long (Psalm 16:10). Jesus predicted His own Resurrection on numerous occasions (Matthew 12:40, 20:18–20; John 2:19).

The divine origin of the Bible is demonstrated through its frequent use of prophecy. Of all the "holy books" of the world, only the Bible contains accurate, predictive prophecy, because only the God of the Bible knows the future and has the power to bring it to pass (Isaiah 46:9–10).

THE BIBLE HOLDS THE
KEY TO
ETERNAL LIFE

OUR GREATEST NEED

Each of us has sinned against God and desperately needs His forgiveness. This need far exceeds all others because your eternal destiny depends on it.

OUR DEEPEST LONGING

Throughout history, people have longed to cheat death and avoid God's judgment, but the fountain of youth does not exist, and unless the Lord returns first, death is inescapable.

THE ONLY ANSWER

The Bible's ultimate message answers our greatest need and meets our deepest yearning. God sent His Son, Jesus Christ, to die in our place, taking our sins upon Himself. Jesus Christ satisfied God's justice, and three days later God raised Him from the dead, demonstrating that He has power over death and giving the hope of eternal life to all who turn from their sins and believe in Him. The answer to our greatest need and deepest longing is the Crucifixion and Resurrection of Jesus Christ.

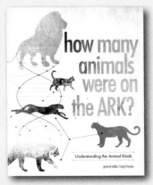

978-0-89051-935-6

978-0-89051-977-6

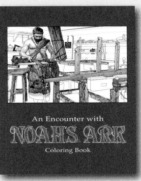

978-0-89051-934-9

978-0-89051-931-8

978-0-89051-936-3

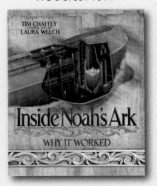

978-0-89051-932-5

SEEING IS BELIEVING

Now you can go behind the scenes and see the dream come together beam by beam in *The Building of the Ark Encounter,* discover the ancient technology and systems that Noah could have used in *Inside Noah's Ark: Why It Worked,* and get answers to the top question asked in *How Many Animals Were on the Ark?* You can also get creative with the *Expedition Ark Journal* and *An Encounter with Noah's Ark* adult coloring book.

VISIT **MASTERBOOKS.COM** — *Where Faith Grows!* — TO SEE OUR FULL LINE OF LICENSED ARK ENCOUNTER PRODUCTS OR CALL 800-999-3777

THINK

BIGGER

ARK
ENCOUNTER

ArkEncounter.com

Williamstown, KY
(south of Cincinnati)